THE LITTLE MINXES.

LONDON: DAVID BOGUE, 86, FLEET STREET.

6.

THE GIRL WHO WOULD NOT LEARN TO SEW.

ow, Nelly, there's a darling girl,
  Do try and hem this handkerchief;
All little girls, as up they grow,
Must learn to hem, and baste, and sew,
  Or they will surely come to grief.

"For you must learn to make your clothes,
  Since none but babes and dolls of wood
By other people's hands are dress'd;
You're not a baby, that's confess'd;
  And for a doll you're far too good."

But Nelly blubbers, pouts, and cries,
  In spite of all Mamma could say;
To make a stitch she would not try,—
  Mamma exclaim'd, with many a sigh—
  "Nelly will be a doll some day!"

Regardless of this dreadful doom,
  Nelly refused to learn to sew;
Her stupid head for nothing good,
Grew more and more like solid wood,
  Her limbs more stiff began to grow.

Her brow grew flat, her eyes grew round,
  Her arms stuck out like matches straight,
Her flesh grew hard as oak or deal,
A stupid smile her lips reveal—
  To be *a doll* is Nelly's fate.

"So," cried Mamma, "to dress Miss Nell
  Is now the easiest thing to do:
Whene'er she wants new shoes or frocks
  We'll fetch the toyman with his box,
    To stick them on with nails and
      glue."

THE GIRL WHO CRIED AFTER HER MAMMA.

IT was very hard that poor Mamma
    Could scarcely step outside the
      door,
But little Jane would quick begin
To scream and bellow with a din
    As loud as any ox's roar.

"Mamma! Mamma! you must not
    go,
    I won't be left alone—Oh dear!
Oh take me with you, I shall die."

The neighbours to their doors would
    fly,
    Thinking that murderers were near.

Now Jane's Mamma was really
    pain'd—
    She could not make a morning call,
Or go to buy her market stock,
For fear her little girl should shock
    The neighbours by her dreadful
    squall.

One day Mamma was forced to go
 On bus'ness out: she formed a plan.
"Jenny," she said, "I'm going out,
You wish to follow me no doubt—
 Don't cry—to-day I think you can.

"You know I've told you many a time
 I can't take little girls with me
To call on friends: they're in the way;
But little *dogs* to bark and play
 Where'er they PLEASE, are always free.

"And so, instead of taking Dash,
 Who always follows at my heels,
You be my little dog to-day,
Wearing his string and collar gay,
While merry little Dash shall stay
 At home, to take your place and
  meals."

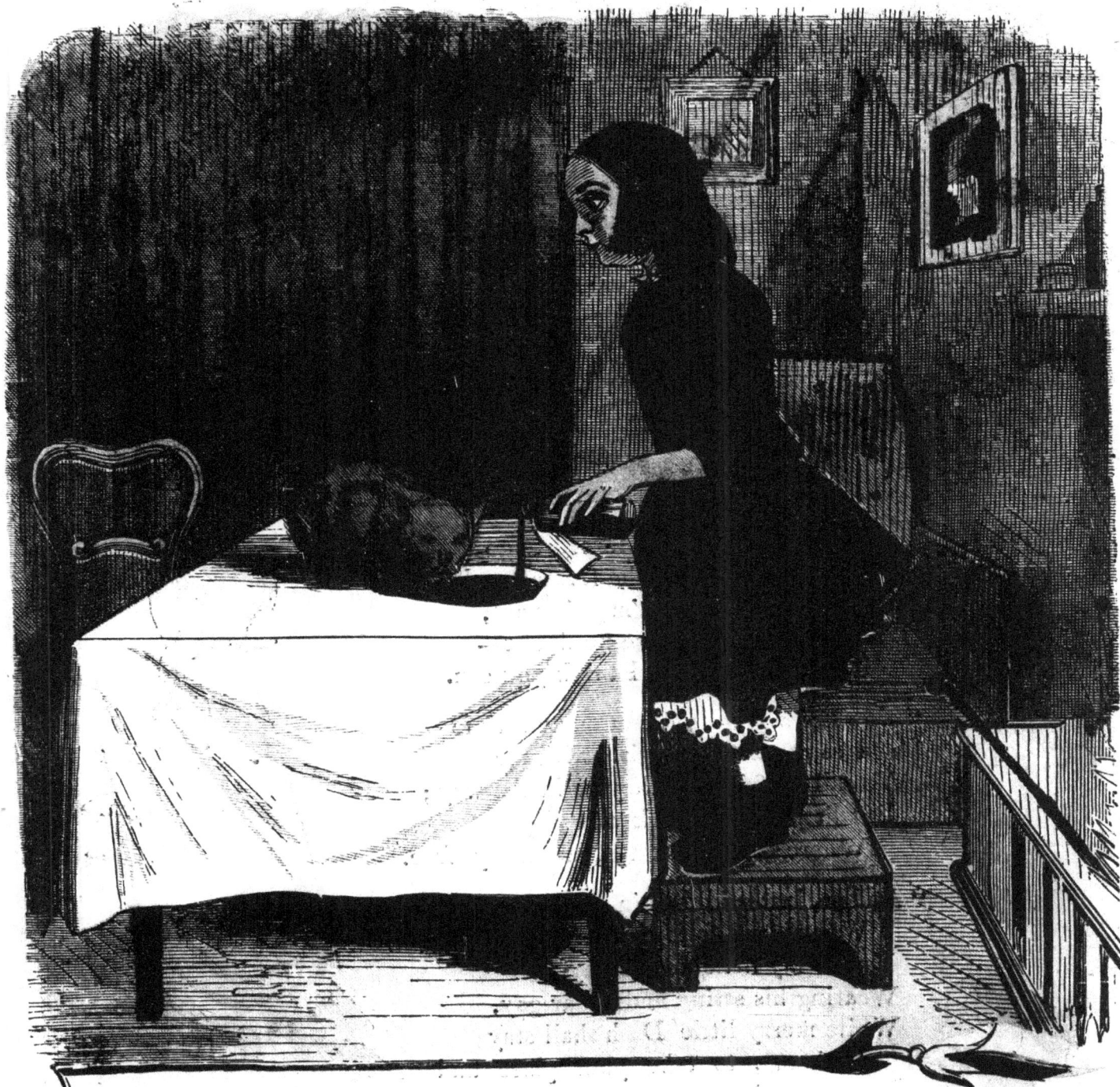

THE GIRL, THE CAT, AND THE PHYSIC.

Miss Polly was poorly,
So was the cat :
Nothing much, surely,
Funny in that.

But the cat got better
As fast as they 'd let her,
And swallow'd her dinner,
While Polly grew thinner,

And day after day, as white
    as a platter,
While day after day Miss
    Pussy got fatter.

None understood it—
    Woman or man!
But you, who have view'd
    it
    In our picture, can.
Miss Polly, who *is* sick,
Hates taking physic;
She vows she has taken it
    (Having well shaken it);
But you see she has pour'd it
    for Puss in a platter,
Who laps it, and quickly
    gets better and fatter.

Thinner and thinner
    Still Polly grew,
Near through the skin her
    Bones peeping show.
Pussy grew stouter,
Frisking about her,
Eating and drinking,
Dozing and blinking,
Still Polly gives Puss her
    draughts in the platter,
So Polly gets thinner, and
    Pussy grows fatter.

Pale as white muslin
    Polly's cheek grows,
Ev'ry one puzzling,—
    Who the truth knows?
Still she grows thinner,
Loathing her dinner;
Pussy grows rounder,
Daily sleeps sounder.

Moral: young ladies who'd
    wish to get fatter,
Take all your physic when
    aught is the matter.

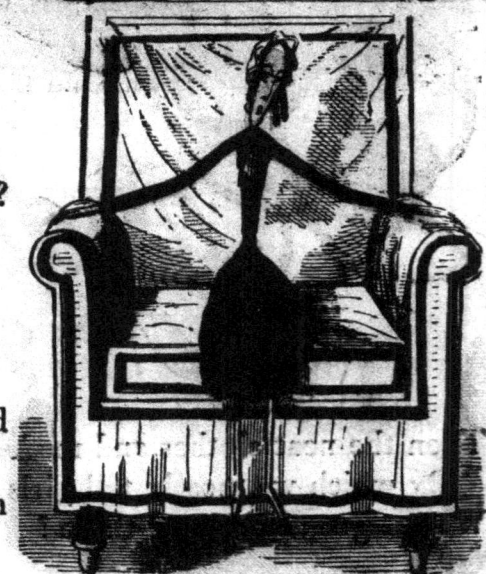

THE TOMBOY.

I.

Heyday!

what's here, a girl or boy?
    In truth, 't is somewhat hard to tell.
A girl 't would seem by frock and hat;
But then—the kite and cricket-bat,
    With marbles and a top as well.

Then the neat clothes and modest look,
    By which we mostly tell girls *from* boys.
What signs are here of these ?   Why, none.

What can it be ?   As sure as fun
I have it—yes !   The creature 's one
    Of those strange beings known as Tomboys!

II

No nicer girl than Lotty Gray,
    Of kinder heart or temper sweeter,
Was ever known. But, well-a-day!
She had one fault: she would not stay
Indoors; but loved in fields to play
    With great rough boys like George
        and Peter.

Now, George and Peter both were good,
    And Lotty did quite right to love
        them.
Yet boys may romp in field or wood
At many games for girls too rude!
But Lotty never understood
    Such rules as these, or felt above
        them.

She would play horses, marbles, base;
    In vain her parents did entreat her
To stop with Sisters Rose and Grace,
To read and write, or stitch and lace.
No! She preferr'd to romp and race
    About the fields with George and
        Peter.

To tell of all Miss Lotty's scrapes,
Her very narrow life-escapes,
(Through playing like a boy) would be
Too hard a task for even me.
But there's one thing I don't believe:
Whate'er she did her friends to grieve,
I don't believe (although they say
The thing was done in open day,
No doubt Miss Lotty to annoy)
She fought young Bill, the butcher's
    boy.

No! I must contradict it flat,
Lotty was ne'er so bad as that.

III.

nother adventure, as sad in its way,
    I fear I must give to the reader,
And own to it's truth. The young lady, one
        day,
    In the woods, with her chosen companions, must
        play,
At a game they call " Follow my Leader.'
George was the leader, and gallantly led
    O'er a stream, which, of slime and mud full,
        rushes.
A log was the bridge.   Peter over it sped,

But Lotty she slipp'd, and fell flop ! over
  head
  'Mong the mud, and the reeds, and
    bullrushes.
Peter and George, they fished her out,
Almost smothered and drenched through-
  out,
    Alack !
    As black
    As a collier's sack,
With the mud that dripp'd from her
  sides and back.
They led her home, and she left a trail
Like the slimy track of a coal-black
  snail.

She mounts the pony, though no one
  is nigh
To save her, if pony should kick or
  shy.
    Pony is vicious,
    With spite pernicious,
He kicks up his heels as a sport deli-
  cious,
And Lotty, toss'd off from his slip-
  pery back, buries
Deep in a thicket of hazel and black-
  berries.
This is her portrait, as out she scram-
  bles,
Torn to pieces by thorns and brambles.

IV.

Lotty's papa had a pony gray;
George had got on his back one day,
    Lotty must try
    With George to vie;

V.

Quite well I remember
One fifth of November:
    To keep up the Gunpowder Plot,
George, Peter, and others,
    Friends, cousins, and brothers,
Had crackers, and squibs, and what not.
Miss Lotty, to help them, must fill her
    pockets
With catherine wheels, blue candles, and
    rockets.

    Flash, crash ! Smash, splash !

Lotty is paid for her conduct rash ;
A spark has caught her firework stock,
She is all in a blaze—hat, petticoats, frock !
George, from a distance, to help her springs,
Peter a bucket of water flings.

    Her clothes in tinder,
    Her hat a cinder,
The water has drench'd, the flame half
    skinn'd her:
With eyebrows singed, and frizzling hair,
They carry her home in the Guy Faux
    chair.

VI.

Now, what became of Lotty Gray?
    You'll never guess, I'll bet a penny.
   'Twas this—as older Lotty grew

She thought she'd just *grow better too*,
   And grew as good a girl as any.
She's left off romping long ago;
   It may sound strange, but still the fact 'tis,
Peter and George she sees at play
Without a tear; she likes to stay

Indoors, to read, or draw, or practise.
Father and Mother both are proud
   Of Lotty now, with reasons ample.
Good bye, young ladies! I have done:
You who have habits bad to shun,
   Follow Miss Lotty's good example.

THE GIRL AND THE LOOKING-GLASS.

Horror! here's a dreadful case!
A little girl with ne'er a face,
  No cheeks, nor eyes, nor nose.
How came she so? The tale, though sad,
I'm forced to tell, to warn the bad
  Before too late it grows.

The little girl whom here you see,
Was once as pretty as could be—
  Her cheeks were like the rose,
Her teeth like beads of iv'ry bright,
Her forehead smooth as marble white,
  Her eyes as black as sloes.

But she was vain! Whole hours, they say,
She spent before the glass each day;
  Till (so the story goes)
One day she'd look'd so long, alas!
Her face remain'd stuck in the glass!
And here my tale must close.

THE GIRL WHO WAS ONLY MADE FOR
SHOW.

F course you remember the story I told
    Of the girl whose delight was to look at herself.
I 've another of one who believed young and old
Cared for nothing but *her* in full dress to behold,
As a wonderful picture in jewels and gold,
    Or a rare vase of flowers stuck up on a shelf.

    She ne'er had done dressing : from morning till night
      She was foraging over each draw'r and each box ;
Whatever she found that was showy and bright,
    She'd put on, never asking who gave her the right,
And (though knowing their cost) of all warning in spite,
    She would constantly wear her best bonnets and frocks.

She'd lounge at the window and strut out of doors,
  Thinking ev'ry one watch'd her with wondering eyes.
She will not learn a lesson, all work she abhors,
She can scarcely tell sevens or sixes from fours,
She despises e'en skipping-ropes, dolls, battledores
  And likes finery better than puddings or pies.
Her Parents were saddened to see her so vain,
  But they hoped for improvement as older she grew;
But the taller she gets, all the more it is plain
She affects the grown woman in pride and disdain:
Though at twelve years of age, in the use of her brain,
  She's as helpless and silly as babies at two!

At last her Papa, fairly sick of her ways,
  Said "It's no use attempting Louise to improve,
She but cares to be stared at by popular gaze,
And for nought else is fit: a new case I will glaze,
And in my curiosity-closet she stays,
  For she's really too vain and too stupid to move."
And so Miss Louise in a glass-case is stuck,
  As a thing to be look'd at 'mongst other things rare:
A mummy, a helmet, the horns of a buck,
Some statues, a stuff'd four-wing'd Muscovy duck,
Coins, butterflies, snakes:—Those who envy her luck,
  Had best do as she did in hopes to get there.

9 JA 58